ROMANS

LECTIO DIVINA FOR YOUTH

ROMANS
LECTIO DIVINA FOR YOUTH

ANCIENT FAITH SERIES

Barefoot Ministries®
Kansas City, Missouri

Copyright © 2009 by Barefoot Ministries®

ISBN: 978-0-8341-5029-4

Printed in the United States of America

Written by Keith Drury

Editor: Mike Wonch
Assistant Editor: Catherine M. Shaffer
Cover Design: J.R. Caines
Interior Design: Sharon Page

Adapted from *Lectio Divina Bible Studies: Listening for God Through Romans.*

Drury, Keith. *Lectio Divina Bible Studies: Listening for God Through Romans.* Indianapolis, IN: Wesleyan Publishing House and Beacon Hill Press of Kansas City, 2006.

Library of Congress Cataloging-in-Publication Data : 2009908228

10 9 8 7 6 5 4 3 2 1

ABOUT THE
LECTIO DIVINA
BIBLE STUDIES

Lectio divina (pronounced lek-tsee-oh dih-vee-nuh), is a Latin phrase that means *sacred reading.* It is the ancient Christian practice of communicating with God through the reading and study of Scripture. Throughout history, great Christian leaders have used and adapted this ancient method of interpreting Scripture.

The idea behind *lectio divina* is to look at a Bible passage in such a way that Bible study becomes less about study and more about listening. The approach is designed to focus our attention on what God is saying to us through the Word. Through the process of *lectio divina* we not only read to understand with our minds, but we read to hear with our hearts and obey. It is a way of listening to God through His Word.

Some throughout history have said that *lectio divina* turns Bible study on its head—normally we read the Bible, but in *lectio divina, the Bible reads us.* That is probably a good way to describe it. It is God using His Word in a conversation with us to read into our lives and speak to our hearts.

In this series, we will use the traditional *lectio divina* model. We have expanded each component so that it can be used by both individuals and by groups. Each session in this study includes the following elements. (Latin words and their pronunciation are noted in parentheses.)

- **Reading** (*Lectio* "lek-tsee-oh"). We begin with a time of quieting ourselves prior to reading. Then we take a slow, careful reading of a passage of Scripture. We focus our minds on the central theme of the passage. When helpful, we read out loud or read the same passage over and over several times.
- **Meditation** (*Meditatio* "medi-tah-tsee-oh"). Next, we explore the meaning of the Bible passage. Here we dig deep to try to un-

derstand all of what God might be saying to us. We think on the passage. We explore the images, and pay attention to the emotions and feelings that the passage provides. We put ourselves in the story. We look for particular words or phrases that leap off the page as the Spirit begins to speak to us through the Word.

- **Prayer** (*Oratio* "or-ah-tsee-oh"). As we meditate on the passage, we respond to God by communicating with Him. We specifically ask God to speak to us through His Word. We begin to dialog with Him about what we have read. We express praise, thanksgiving, confession, or agreement to God. And we listen. We wait before Him in silence, allowing God the chance to speak.

- **Contemplation** (*Contemplatio* "con-tehm-plah-tsee-oh"). At this point in our conversation through the Word, we come to a place where we rest in the presence of God. Our study is now about receiving what He has said to us. Imagine two old friends who have just talked at length—and now without words, they just sit together and enjoy each other's presence. Having spent time listening to God, we know a little better how God is shaping the direction of our lives. Here there is a yielding of oneself to God's will. We resolve to act on the message of Scripture.

GROUP STUDY

This book is designed to be useful for both individual and group study. To use this in a group, you may take one of several approaches:

- **Individual Study/Group Review**. Make sure each member of the group has a copy of the book. Have them read through one section during the week. (They will work through the same passage or portions of it each day that week.) Then, when you meet together, review what thoughts, notes, and insights the members of the group experienced in their individual study. Use the group questions at the end of the section as a guide.

- **Group Lectio**. Make sure each member of the group has a copy of the book. Have them read through one section during the week in individual study. When you meet together as a group, you will study the passage together through a reading form similar to lectio divina:

- ○ **First, read the passage out loud several times to the group**. Group members respond by waiting in silence and letting God speak.
- ○ **Second, have the passage read aloud again to the group once or twice more**. Use different group members for different voices, and have them read slowly. Group members listen for a word or two that speaks to them, and share it with the group. Break into smaller groups if appropriate.
- ○ **Third, read the passage out loud again, and have the group pray together to ask God what He might be saying to each person, and to the group as a whole**. Go around and share what each person is learning from this process. At this point, review together the group questions at the end of the section.[1]
- • **Lectio Divina Steps for Groups**. Make sure each member has a copy of the book. As a group, move through the study together, going through each of the parts: reading, mediation, prayer, and contemplation. Be sure to use the group questions at the end of the section.

The important thing about using *lectio divina* in a group is to remember that this is to be incarnational ("in the flesh")—in other words, we begin to live out the Word in our community. We carry God's Word in us, (in the flesh, or incarnate in us) and we carry that Word into our group to be lived out among them.

The *Lectio Divina Bible Studies* invite readers to slow down, read Scripture, meditate upon it, and prayerfully respond to God's Word.

---

1. Parts of the "Group Lectio" section adapted from Tony Jones, *The Sacred Way: Spiritual Practices for Everyday Life*, Grand Rapids: Zondervan, 2005, p. 54.

CONTENTS

INTRODUCTION

For many Christians, an introduction to Romans comes early in their faith journeys. Pastors frequently use key verses from this book of the Bible to lead people to faith in Christ. For example in 3:23, we see that no one is free from the sin problem. In 6:23, we see that the punishment for sin is always death. Through the death of Jesus, however, God offers the free gift of a new way—life that lasts forever. In 10:9-10, we see that the way to receive this gift is by confessing belief in Jesus Christ and in the fact that God resurrected Him—proving His deity and His ultimate power over death.

The Book of Romans (a letter written by Paul to the church at Rome, 1:7) is richer yet for the experienced believer—the believer who may be stressed-out by opposition, who may feel distant from God due to circumstances, who may be worn down by the battle. Who can forget the energizing words of Romans 8:38-39: "For I am convinced that neither death nor life, neither angels nor demons, neither the present nor the future, nor any powers, neither height nor depth, nor anything else in all creation, will be able to separate us from the love of God that is in Christ Jesus our Lord"?

Paul wrote this letter to a church he'd never visited. He longed to meet these believers in person, but at this stage in his third missionary journey (described in Acts 15—21), the severe opposition he was meeting among the Jews, particularly in Jerusalem, made him unsure that he'd ever reach Rome. For this reason, he wrote this letter that so beautifully describes the universal truth of salvation by faith for Jews and Gentiles together.

It is a reasoned, intelligent argument of the whole message of the gospel. A favorite of believers down through the centuries, including Martin Luther[2] who called it "the very purest Gospel," this letter to the Romans is worthy of study and appreciation by all who seek the salvation and comfort of God.

---

2. Martin Luther (1483—1546)—a German theologian, monk, and church reformer whose teachings began the Protestant Reformation. He is the founder of the Lutheran Church.

RELATIONSHIPS AND REVELATIONS
LISTENING FOR GOD THROUGH ROMANS 1:8-25

SUMMARY

Even before creation, there were relationships—between God the Father, Son, and Holy Spirit. The Trinity (God the Father, Son, and Holy Spirit) loves and communes with one other. God, by His very nature, is relational. Then we came on the scene. God created and relates to us, and He inspires love between His children. Paul loved the Roman church and longed to be with them. Today's church is a loving community of relationships that reflects (in its best moments) the love among the Godhead. The Church is relational, in the image of God.

How can we relate to God if we don't know Him? We can only know Him because He has made himself known. He revealed himself through "natural revelation"—in nature and in human conscience. No person born on earth can say, "I never heard." We have no excuse, since we all are witnesses of God through nature. The blowing wind. A newborn baby's cry. A field of flowers in full bloom.

Nature isn't even the best picture of God ever taken, though. Jesus Christ is—He is Revelation with a capital "R," *the* Revelation of God. In Jesus Christ, we meet *very God*. When we enter a relationship with Christ, we enter a relationship with the Godhead and with the family of God, for none can call God "Father" who does not call the Church "Brother" and "Sister."

PREPARATION ☦ FOCUS YOUR THOUGHTS

What person do you long to see who is far away?

What group of people whom you've never met would you like to visit?

Share about a time when you felt closer to God when in nature.

READING ☦ HEAR THE WORD

When we read Romans, we are "looking over the shoulders" of the first-century, conservative Jewish Christians who received the letter. It is perhaps the most orderly attempt in the New Testament at answering the questions conservative, deep-thinking Christian Jews would be asking about the gospel. The way of salvation to a Jew prior to Christ's life, death, and resurrection had been clear: *We are God's chosen people; the Law[3] was given to us; we attempt to obey the Law; sacrifices and rituals provide atonement for our sins where we miss the mark (Leviticus 6:8—7:18); and righteousness[4] comes by obedience to God's commands.*

Paul preached a different kind of gospel: *a righteousness that came through faith by grace due to Christ's own once-for-all sacrifice on the Cross.* It is no wonder conservative, well-behaved Jewish Christians might resist Paul's new teaching. Would people "saved by faith in Christ and not obedience to the Law" then abandon any commitment to holy living? Was the Law useless? Why did God give the Law if He was going to make the Law invalid? Was being the "chosen people" wasted? Does the coming of Christ destroy the Old Testament?

Romans 1 is the preface to this wonderful book—perhaps the greatest attempt by Paul to explain the gospel[5] in a way that satisfies the human mind. Read this first section of Romans as

---

3. For the Jewish person in Paul's day the Law would be the first five books of the Old Testament, referred to as the Torah. The main focus of the Law would be the Ten Commandments.

4. Righteousness is the quality or condition of being right or good. The righteous are people who live righteous lives. The righteous are people who live in right relation to God. Thus, the righteous are people who have been justified by God. (Eby, J. Wesley, ed. *A Dictionary of the Bible & Christian Doctrine in Everyday English.* Kansas City: Beacon Hill Press of Kansas City, 2004), p. 253-254.

5. The gospel is the good news about Jesus Christ. Gospel is from the Greek word *evangel*, which means "the good news of victory." The victory of Jesus over sin has made salvation possible for all people. This is the message of the gospel. It is a message that God loves sinners and wants to forgive them. He wants them to be free from sin and spiritual death. (Eby, J. Wesley, ed. *A Dictionary of the Bible & Christian Doctrine in Everyday English.* Kansas City: Beacon Hill Press of Kansas City, 2004), p. 119.

if you were opening a letter from the famed and loved apostle Paul—read it as a letter.

MEDITATION ✞ ENGAGE THE WORD

Meditate on Romans 1:8-17

What are some of the verbs Paul uses to express his relationship with the Roman church in this passage? What do they tell us about Paul's relationship with these people?

Describe Paul's relationship with the Romans. Though Paul had not yet visited the Roman church, he apparently already knew many in the church. Glance over his farewell in Romans 15:1-16 to find hints describing the sort of people who got the letter of Romans.

What was the Roman church "famous" for across the then-known world? While our intention should never be fame, what sort of things today could get a church a reputation for famous faith?

Paul claimed to serve God with his "whole heart"—a heart fully devoted to following Jesus Christ. What does it mean to be a half-hearted Christian? How can a half-hearted Christian become whole-hearted?

The Roman Christians were already believers, yet Paul longs to preach the gospel to them that is "the power of God unto salvation." Today we think of preaching the gospel as something to do for unbelievers. What value is it for *believers* to hear the gospel message?

Reflect on the quote by Pope John Paul II. What does it mean to have a righteousness *by faith?* How do we live by faith in our daily lives?

> Faith leads us beyond ourselves. It leads us directly to God.   —Pope John Paul II

Meditate on Romans 1:18-20

We don't like to talk about the "wrath of God," but Paul saw God's wrath already being revealed. Does God reveal His wrath today? If so, to whom does He do this and why?

Think about the quote on God's wrath by Joseph Ratzinger. Close your eyes and visualize this picture in your mind—a raging river into which people determine to walk. How would seeing God's wrath this way change our views?

> The wrath of God is a way of saying that I have been living in a way that is contrary to the love that is God. Anyone who begins to live and grow away from God, who lives away from what is good, is turning his life toward wrath.   —Joseph Ratzinger

The clearest revelation of God is in Jesus Christ, of course, not nature, but God has already revealed himself in creation, making all humans accountable for the revelation they have received. What does nature tell us about God?

Paul argues that all humans are accountable due to this "natural revelation," so they have no excuses when they face the judgment. Think about yourself—what have *you* heard that makes you more accountable than those who have only natural revelation?

Meditate on the quote by William Cowper. How does nature fall short of telling us the full story of God? What does Jesus Christ reveal about God that is far more complete than the revelation of nature?

> Nature is a good name for an effect whose cause is God. —William Cowper

Meditate on 1:21-25

How might a person know God yet not glorify Him? How did the idolaters of this passage know God?

How bad must it get before God gives people over to their own sinfulness, in a sense letting them go to the logical end of their path? This passage seems to be more about a people than a person. Does God abandon nations? tribes? denominations? local churches? Can you think of any time in biblical history where God seemed to withdraw from a people and let them continue on their sinful path—at least for a time?

PRAYER ✟ ASK AND LISTEN

Seek the face of God. Ask, "Lord, what are You saying to us today?"

In group sentence prayers, first *praise* God for the beauty of creation, and then *thank* Him for Jesus Christ's revelation, and finally *ask* Him to help your church illustrate loving relationships.

CONTEMPLATION ✟ REFLECT AND YIELD

If God has best revealed himself in Jesus, what should you do to know more about what Jesus Christ was like?

GROUP STUDY

- What about the gospel message might tempt a Christian to be "ashamed" or embarrassed by it?

- Has there ever been a time when you were too embarrassed or ashamed to share the gospel message. If so, how did this experience make you feel?

- How does nature reveal to you the character of God? Are there ways in which nature falls short in explaining the full range of who God is?

- How can we daily glorify God and thank Him for who He is and all He does? How can we avoid futile (useless) thinking (v. 21)?

- What are the ways we can seek the wisdom and truth of God in our everyday lives?

- Take time to think about all the ways you can serve God this coming week.

NOTHING IN MY HAND
I BRING
LISTENING FOR GOD THROUGH ROMANS 3:9-31

SUMMARY

In Romans 1 as Paul is describing the nasty sins of the Gentiles, you can imagine his Jewish readers nodding their heads with condemning amens. In the next chapter, though, he reminds the Jews that they, too, are sinners. Thus they, too, have no excuse. Paul does begin chapter 3 by admitting some advantages to being a Jew (they had Scripture, etc.), but ultimately there is none righteous—not one, because all have sinned, both Jew and Gentile.

Paul paints the Jews in the same light as the Gentiles: sinners desperately in need of God's grace. He writes Romans in order to announce a new way to be righteous. Keeping the Law was one way, but nobody could do it perfectly. This new path to righteousness is through faith in Christ. If our righteousness comes from God through Christ alone, we have nothing to boast about but Jesus Christ and God's mercy.

PREPARATION ☦ FOCUS YOUR THOUGHTS

Think about a time when you had absolutely no hope to solve a problem with your own resources—you were completely helpless and had to trust someone else to pull you through. Think about another time when you tried to fix something on your own but only made it worse.

READING ☦ HEAR THE WORD

After outlining the absolute hopelessness of the Gentiles to be righteous (in chap. 1), Paul then includes the Jews (in chap. 2), for they were just as hopelessly unable to keep the Jewish law. So both Gentiles and Jews are in the same boat: sinking in hopeless and inadequate self-righteousness. The obvious response from the conservative Jewish Christians was, "then what advantage has there been in being a Jew at all?" In chapter 3, Paul responds to that question. The Jews had the Law; they had Scriptures; they understood sin and holiness, but ultimately what good did it do them, since they couldn't live up to the expectations?

When Paul quotes the Old Testament to prove the universality of unrighteousness, he quotes it from memory—thus he sometimes paraphrases the original words. This common rabbinic method of stringing together a series of quotes from Scripture to make a point is called a *charaz*—literally "stringing pearls."

Christians sometimes wrongly believe that the Old Testament God was a God of the Jewish nation and that Jesus came to present a God of all people. This is not so. The Old Testament Jews considered "the God of the Jews" to be the One True God of the entire world.

Read the entire section of Scripture aloud with forcefulness, as if you are a lawyer making a case before a jury.

MEDITATION 🕇 ENGAGE THE WORD

Meditate on Romans 3:9-20

What were the advantages the Jews had over the Gentiles before Jesus came? What advantages do people raised in the church have today? Yet, even though some groups start off with what seems like advantages, in what ways are we all absolutely equal?

Paul strung together like pearls at least five psalms and a verse from Isaiah in his poetic description of human nature gone sour without Christ. Which of these are matters of character? behavior? tongue?

The Jews cherished the commandments and the Law hoping they might become righteous by keeping all the rules. Paul blasts this hope in the concluding verse of this section by citing the real purpose of the commandments and law.

Reflect on the quote by Paul. How do the words of Paul written to the Ephesians relate to what he says to the Romans? Can we achieve righteousness through our works (actions)? What is the relationship between faith and works?

> *For it is by grace you have been saved, through faith—and this not from yourselves, it is the gift of God—not by works, so that no one can boast.*
>
> *—Paul (Ephesians 2:8-9)*

Meditate on Romans 3:21-26

Paul describes two ways to be righteous; *Keeping all the rules* or *trusting Christ by faith*. The first focuses on what we can do for ourselves, the second on what God can do for us (and has already done). The first route is hopeless, but the second has been revealed in Jesus Christ.

Read the C. S. Lewis quote on page 25. The dictionary says that "spuriously" means: Lacking authenticity or validity in essence or origin; not genuine; false.[6] In light of this, what is a "spuriously good conscience?" How can good people more easily trust their goodness to count for something? Rules often focus on the "don'ts" of Christian living rather than the "do's." If we were to have more rules for the dos, what might they be?

---

6. <http://www.thefreedictionary.com/spuriously>. Accessed May 11, 2009.

> Nothing gives one a more spuriously good conscience
> than keeping rules, even if there has been a total ab-
> sence of all real charity and faith.   —C. S. Lewis

Paul argues that God was demonstrating His justice by pro-
viding Jesus Christ as a means to righteousness. When we re-
pent of our sins God justifies us by His grace through faith.
That is, we are forgiven, made right, and stand before God, a
new creation in a new relationship with God. Why is faith so
important?

Meditate on Romans 3:27-31

How do we appear to boast of our goodness to others, to
God, or even privately to ourselves?

Think about Paul's whole argument here—being righteous by
grace through faith alone and not through our own goodness.
So then we don't have to keep the law? Paul's answer: faith
does not invalidate the law, but upholds it. What do you think
he meant (v. 31)?

Think about the verse from the Charles Wesley hymn, "O for
a Thousand Tongues." We're familiar with individuals casting
their hope on Christ for righteousness, but can a *nation* do
this? If a nation (or a church or any other group of people)
were to trust Christ for righteousness (not just to help them

win wars, but truly trust Christ for righteousness), how would
a *group* do this?

> *Look unto him, ye nations, own Your God, ye fallen race;*
> *Look, and be saved through faith alone, Be justified by*
> *grace. See all your sins on Jesus laid: The Lamb of God*
> *was slain, His soul was once an offering made For*
> *every soul of man.* —Charles Wesley
> *("O for a Thousand Tongues")*

PRAYER ☦ ASK AND LISTEN

Seek the face of God. Ask, "Lord, what are You saying to us
today?"

Pray, thanking God for His unmerited favor—the grace He
freely gives to all of us, though we are undeserving.

CONTEMPLATION ☦ REFLECT AND YIELD

Think about the gospel that grants righteousness by faith and
not by our performance. Take some time to journal your
thoughts about ways to submit to this great plan of salvation.

GROUP STUDY

- Have you every tried to earn your salvation through good and right actions? How did that experience leave you feeling?

- What does the fact that you *can't* earn your salvation mean to your life?

- What is the difference between keeping rules and trusting rule-keeping?

- Discuss the following words: *righteousness, faith, grace,* and *justified.* How would you define each word? What does each word mean to the life of a non-Christian? What does each word mean to the life of a Christian?

- Make a list of everything you could offer as evidence that you are a good person, then put the list in a place you pass by often. Whenever you pass that place, recall the true source of righteousness.

CHOOSING OUR SLAVE MASTER

LISTENING FOR GOD THROUGH
ROMANS 6:11-23; 7:14-24

SUMMARY

Paul argued that all have sinned. The Jews were caretakers of the Law, but it didn't really help them be righteous, for nobody can keep the Law perfectly. Jews and Gentiles alike are under condemnation. The Jewish Law didn't help them get off the hook.

Jesus brought with Him a new way to be righteous—by faith, not by keeping the Law. We were once slaves to sin, but now we are freed from sin and are slaves to Christ. Paul leaves us no in-between position: we are either slaves to sin or slaves to Christ. We can't serve both masters. If we are slaves to sin, we can't be good even if we want to. And if we are slaves to Christ, we can't keep on sinning. It is slavery either way: so sin or to Christ. Our choice is which master to serve.

PREPARATION ⚜ FOCUS YOUR THOUGHTS

Discuss how each of the following groups of people can be free, and yet not free: children, college students, single adults, young married couples without children, divorced adults, empty nesters, and aged nursing home residents.

Imagine what a person would be like who was absolutely and totally free.

READING ⚜ HEAR THE WORD

Before reading, capture the flow of the context. Paul's points so far are as follows: (1) No one is righteous (neither Jew nor Gentile) since all have sinned and need grace; (2) Jesus brought a new way to be righteous—by faith through God's grace; (3) Abraham himself was even justified by faith (chap. 4) by trusting God's promise (which was credited to him as righteousness); (4) God demonstrated His love for us when Christ died at just the right time; (5) sin entered the world through Adam, but life and righteousness centered through Jesus Christ, the new Adam; and (6) what Adam ruined, Christ restores.

The question behind chapter 6 is if we're saved by grace through faith and not works, couldn't we keep on sinning? Paul's answer: By no means! We are either slaves to sin or Christ. If we serve Christ, we can't keep on sinning. Taking on the part of an unbeliever, Paul describes a person in slavery to sin who can't do the good he knows is right and can't avoid the sin he knows is wrong. Chapter 8 is the hopeful glorious end to the matter, but we cover that in the next chapter.

Have two people read these sections of Scripture—the first reading the selection from chapter 6 with a reasoned, logical voice and the second reading the selection from chapter 7 with emotion and deep feeling.

MEDITATION ☦ ENGAGE THE WORD

Meditate on Romans 6:11-14

To Paul, what would a Christian do to "let sin reign" in his/her life? Ponder the "do nots" or "shall nots" in this passage, then describe what sort of lifestyle a Christian is supposed to have related to sin and sinning.

Paul will later address offering our bodies to God (12:1-2), but here he plants the idea of "offering parts of your body to sin." Think about how some body parts might be offered to sin. Now, think about how those body parts might be offered to God.

What does it mean that "sin shall not be your master?" How much sinning can a Christian commit before being mastered by sin? What percentage of people today would agree with John Chrysostom's quote on page 32?

Men have the power of thinking that they may avoid
sin.   *—John Chrysostom*

Meditate on Romans 6:15-23

Paul was accused of preaching that salvation by faith meant
Christians could live any way they wanted, and Paul's church in
Corinth gave some credence to that accusation. Paul defends
his gospel against that charge. Find and read the phrases where
he rejects the charge that he is preaching a "sinning religion."

Paul alludes to the past sins these Roman Christians were
now ashamed of. What are some sins people who are now
saved might be ashamed of?

Find and repeat all the phrases in this passage that are past
tense: *were, used to, have been,* etc. Then find and repeat all
the phrases that are present tense: *are, now, have, become,* etc.
From this exercise, what picture emerges of Christian life related to sinning? What is the meaning of the Ralph Waldo
Emerson quote on sin and grace?

Think, and be careful what thou art within; For there is
sin in the desire of sin; Think, and be thankful, in a dif-
ferent case; For there is grace in the desire of grace.
                                    —Ralph Waldo Emerson

In Romans 6:23, Paul's discussion of the relationship of sin and human beings points toward the destination of the two slaveries. What meaning do you get from this verse?

Meditate on Romans 7:14-24

This passage may be the most misunderstood passage of Scripture. Paul employs a rhetorical device here when using the first person "I," as a parent might do when preparing a high school senior for college. "OK, the alarm goes off again, but I've stayed up late, so I hit the snooze button and forget going to classes; soon I'm flunking out." Paul here describes the life of the slave of sin using first-person rhetoric. Read the section slowly, phrase by phrase, with this thought in mind: to better understand his role as a pre-Christian sinner.

Many Christian down through history have taken this passage to describe an in-between state of a Christian—a person saved but not yet "entirely sanctified."[7] Do you see this passage more as describing the struggles of someone who has not yet become a Christian, or someone who is a Christian but not yet entirely sanctified?

---

7. a) Entire Sanctification is the gift of God that replaces our self-centeredness with Christ-centeredness.

b) It is received by faith in a moment of time, the same way we receive regeneration.

c) It is like stepping through a door into a room of growth, which continues for the rest of our lives.

(Moore, Frank. *More Coffee Shop Theology*. Kansas City: Beacon Hill Press of Kansas City, 1998), p. 70-71.

Think about the Hungarian Proverb. Sin entered the world when Adam made the decision to eat the apple. Although it has been thousands of years since Adam chose to disobey God, how do we still feel the effects of that first sin? How do Christians deal with sin differently from non-Christians?

> *Adam ate the apple, and our teeth still ache.*
> —*Hungarian Proverb*

PRAYER ♱ ASK AND LISTEN

Seek the face of God. Ask, "Lord, what are You saying to us today?"

Pray sentence-prayers of gratitude and praise for being freed from slavery to sin.

CONTEMPLATION ♱ REFLECT AND YIELD

While a Christian is not a slave to sin but to Christ, in what ways are some parts of your body being tempted to return to slavery to sin? Consider your ears, mouth, and mind for starters.

GROUP STUDY

- Spiritually speaking, what does it mean to be brought back from death to life?

- What are the characteristics of someone who is a slave to sin?

- What are the characteristics of someone who is a slave to Christ?

- Why does Paul use the word "wages" for sin and the word "gift" for eternal life in Christ?

- How can a life surrendered to Christ and guided by the Holy Spirit avoid the struggles described by Paul in Romans 7:14-24?

- Write on a 3 x 5 index card 3 ways you can offer your body as a living sacrifice to God this week. Put the card somewhere where you will see it often.

HOPE IN HARD TIMES
LISTENING FOR GOD THROUGH
ROMANS 8:18-39

SUMMARY

Paul was suffering and had experienced suffering all through his ministry. So were the Roman Christians. They faced opposition and persecution for their faith. Here in this chapter, Paul puts his and their present sufferings into perspective—in the light of future glory and hope. Compared to what we will experience in the future and what Christ experienced in the past, our present sufferings don't even make it on the comparison graph.

Paul sets out what will become the song of thousands of future Christians who face suffering—he encourages them and us to become "more than conquerors" in trials and tribulations. We may be stripped of social status, influence, possessions and life itself, but we Christians will be rich anyway; Christ died for us. We have the Spirit within helping us pray. Christ is in heaven interceding for us; and nothing in heaven, on earth, or even under the earth can separate us from God's love. Face it—if God is for us, who can be against us?

PREPARATION ♯ Focus Your Thoughts

The labor-birth sequence is a wonderful example of perspective—given the glory of a new birth, the pains of the moment melt away. What other example of gain-after-pain can you think of?

READING ♯ Hear the Word

In the preceding chapter, Paul sets up the argument by describing a person in bondage to the law of sin and death—unable to do what he knows is right and to resist doing what he knows as wrong. It is a description of wretched slavery to sin that ends with a cry for deliverance: "Who will deliver me from this body of death?" The answer is Jesus Christ, and chapter 8 describes the rescue in such glorious terms that it is hard to read it without responding by singing grateful praise to God. We are free of the law of sin and can obey Christ because we are controlled by the Spirit. Thus, we put to death the deeds of sin as children of God, and we prepare for future glory where even our bodies will be redeemed. When we pray, the Spirit helps us pray. With all this in mind, we can face anything; with God for us who can be against us? Nothing can separate us from God's love.

Arrange for someone to practice reading the entire chapter of Romans 8 as a dramatic reading. Don't follow along in your Bible in a studious manner, but rather listen to the Word the way it was heard in the first century—by hearing it read to an entire church gathering. It will be almost impossible not to feel blessed by these glorious words.

MEDITATION ☦ ENGAGE THE WORD

Meditate on Romans 8:18-27

Paul observed that "the Fall" corrupted both human beings and the creation itself. Since humanity is fallen, how much do we "let it be" and live with the fallenness of humans? How much do we resist it? How would creation—the environment—be different if there had been no Fall? In the meantime, how much should Christians try to help God reverse the effects of the Fall in their own lives? in creation?

Paul presents both creation and humans as "groaning" for deliverance from the Fall. Yet as we groan, we have hope for future deliverance because we have a deposit or the firstfruits of the Holy Spirit.

Not only does creation groan for deliverance from the Fall (as we join in), but the Holy Spirit groans, too—interceding for us "with groans that words cannot express." Tell about some past feelings you have had that words could not express, times when "unintelligible groaning" (out loud or under your breath) was the best way to convey the emotion. What do you feel so deeply about that when you try to express it, your feelings are closer to groans than words?

Read church father Augustine's quote on Christ's suffering. With eyes closed, repeat what Jesus might have thought or said during His suffering—both what He actually said and what He could have thought. Say these words aloud around the circle. Then ponder in silence Christ's sufferings (don't *discuss* them —*ponder* them). Let meaning come to you from God. Then open your eyes, and share the meaning you got from this meditation on Christ's suffering.

> God had one Son on earth without sin, but never one
> without suffering.   —Augustine

Meditate on Romans 8:28-30

How would the Romans have applied the idea that God works in all things for good? What did God want us to get? How does this approach play out in a worldview? How does it apply to earthquakes and hurricanes? to cancer? Apply it to the suffering the Roman Christians and Paul were experiencing.

Read Jim Watkins's quote on page 41 on the "context" and the "why" of Romans 8:28. Discuss how "all things" can be worked toward the end of conforming us to be more like Christ. What are some of the uses of this verse that fall short of its deeper meaning?

> *I had never noticed the verse that followed Romans 8:28 . . . Yep, I had missed the whole "purpose" of Romans 8:28: "To be conformed to the likeness of his Son . . ."*
> —Jim Watkins

Meditate on the verbs of "God's Great Arrangement" for the Church (vv. 29-30): *foreknew, predestined, conformed, called, justified, glorified.* How would you explain the message of these verses to someone else?

Meditate on Romans 8:31-39

What are some charges that might have been brought against the Romans? Paul? yourself? How does Jesus Christ intercede for us differently than the Holy Spirit's intercession a few verses before?

When we are suffering, we tend to think God doesn't love us. Think about the words written by Frederick Lehman. Then, sing together whatever songs come to mind. As you sing, let your heart hear these words of God in Scripture and song. What did God say to you just now?

> *The love of God is greater far Than tongue or pen can ever tell; It goes beyond the highest star, And reaches to the lowest hell.*
> —Frederick M. Lehman

PRAYER ⚜ ASK AND LISTEN

Seek the face of God. Ask, "Lord, what are You saying to us today?"

Sit in attentive silence to hear God's direct word to you on suffering, hope, and His love. When you hear it, speak it aloud in first person—in the tense God would use in speaking to you.

CONTEMPLATION ⚜ REFLECT AND YIELD

God's Word calls for submission—what truth has He given you from this Scripture?

GROUP STUDY

- How will you think differently about suffering and difficulty starting this week? How will you think differently about God's love?

- What is our hope as Christians?

- How does a person know he or she has the Holy Spirit? What evidence is there?

- How do you understand the phrase "work out for the good?"

- How do we know that God is for us? Share an example from your life where you felt God was for you.

- What does it mean to live life with a "more than conquerors through him who loved us" attitude?

- Paul says that there is *nothing* that can separate us from the love of God. How will this truth help in your Christian life this week?

"ALL WHO CALL"— WHO CAN BE SAVED?

LISTENING FOR GOD THROUGH ROMANS 10:1-15

SUMMARY

The Book of Romans is an elaborate, logical argument describing how salvation by faith applies to the Jews and Gentiles alike. Paul's argument is made to Jews and includes some startling points. Chapter 9 is an example of this. Paul has just argued that a sovereign God could do anything He wants—harden Pharaoh's heart or make clay vessels for any purpose, noble or ignoble. Since God can do whatever He wants, who are the Jews to say He can't invite Gentiles on the basis of faith?

In the chapter before us, Paul continues the argument that both Jews and Gentiles are saved by faith. It is easy to see the Jews as stubborn in their refusal to receive this easier way to righteousness, but are we much better? Do we really believe our salvation is by faith alone? *Really?*

PREPARATION ✟ FOCUS YOUR THOUGHTS

Though we easily affirm the idea of "salvation is by faith
through grace alone," what do we often tend to add under our
breath as the small print when considering another person's
salvation?

READING ✟ HEAR THE WORD

There are two kinds of Jews to consider when reading Romans. First are the *Jewish Christians.* These were converted
Jews who followed Christ and were in the church at Rome.
They were likely the "conservative wing" of the church, hoping for holy living and greater emphasis on devotion and
piety. These conservative Christian Jews may have continued
keeping their lifelong convictions carried over from Judaism,
including refusal to eat meat that had been sacrificed to idols
and careful observance of the Sabbath. They held a reverence
for the Law and did not want to see it flicked away as irrelevant.

While they had faith in Christ, they may have been worried
that too much emphasis on grace and faith might open the
door to all kinds of sinful living in the church. Thus they were
cautious about Paul's teaching and its effect, though they
were not obstinate.

However, there is a second group of Jews—the *Israelites.*
These were the Jews through history and in Paul's time who

refused to believe. While Paul intertwines these two groups throughout Romans, it is predominantly this second group he addresses in this section of Romans.

Read the section twice today, verse-by-verse, around the circle—the first time for practice and the second time as a formal reading.

MEDITATION ✝ ENGAGE THE WORD

Meditate on Romans 10:1-4

Paul's heart's desire and prayer focused on the Israelites' salvation. What person do you focus on for salvation? What *group* of people?

What was the knowledge the Jews lacked accompanying their passion? Without using names, describe someone zealous who lacks adequate knowledge. Again, without using names, describe someone knowledgeable who is passionless. Name a person you think is a good example of a balanced, "knowledgeable yet zealous" Christian.

Discuss Colorado preacher John Swanger's quote on page 48 describing the dangers of stagnancy or hysteria. Which side does your church tilt toward? What can a church do to correct an imbalance one way or the other?

> *Knowledge without passion becomes stagnant; passion*
> *without knowledge is just hysteria.   —John E. Swanger*

Paul accused the Jews of trying to establish their own right-eousness rather than receiving righteousness from God. How do we today tend toward this error? How is getting your righteousness from God a matter of submission? What are the potential dangers of this truth?

Meditate on Romans 10:5-13

Paul alludes to the *nearness* of salvation, reminding us we do not have to go up to heaven nor travel down to death to fetch its meaning. What other Scriptures does God bring to mind that also remind us we needn't go to extravagant means to find salvation or truth?

Think about Beatrice Breck's quote about obedience and love. Relate it to what you know of parenting. In what ways do your parents inspire love that prompts obedience?

> *As for obedience and love, the mistake the Jews made*
> *(and many Christians as well) was to try to get to love*
> *through the door of obedience rather than entering in-*
> *to obedience through the doorway of love. Loving God*
> *leads to keeping His commandments, not the reverse.*
> *   —Beatrice Breck*

Read Acts 17:27, and ponder Paul's comment in Athens. Now ponder the nearness of God. Is God near to *everybody* or only some? Is He near to people who have never heard? Is God already near to unbelieving people we work with and live beside?

What are the "two spiritual laws" in this section—what two things must one do to be saved? Meditate on the terms *confess* and *believe*, then visualize the following four words in a four-way diagram in your mind—*believe, heart, confess, mouth.* What does God say to you through this diagram?

How long can a person believe in his/her heart without confessing with his/her mouth? Turn to John 19:38 for more clarity. Think about the Beau Hummel quote. Share this thought with anyone you know who was a secret disciple for a while.

> Secret discipleship is only a temporary condition; sooner or later the secrecy will destroy the discipleship or the discipleship will destroy the secrecy.
>
> —Beau Hummel

Find, then think about these three words in this section: *anyone, all, everyone.* What hymns or choruses do they remind you of? What other Scriptures? What insights does God give you through these words in their context?

Paul here makes the astonishing claim, "There is no difference between Jew and Gentile." Today this concept is obvious to us. However, imagine yourself a Jew in that day receiving this truth. How might you have responded? What other barriers between peoples did Paul melt down elsewhere? Can you find those Scriptures?

Meditate on Romans 10:14-15

Organize in forward sequence the five "salvation process verbs" in verse 14 *(call, believe, hear, preaching, sent)*. Meditate on each word, listening for God's thoughts. Share them with your group. Try to tell your own salvation story using this five-point outline.

PRAYER ⚜ ASK AND LISTEN

Seek the face of God. Ask, "Lord, what are You saying to us today?"

Of all the verses studied, which phrases does God bring back to your mind now as you quietly spend moments in attentive prayer?

CONTEMPLATION ⚜ REFLECT AND YIELD

Articulate what God is saying to you personally today through these Scriptures. Offer what He *may* be saying to your church or group.

Group Study

- Examine your own spiritual life: Do you have a good balance of knowledge and passion?

- Share about some of the extravagant lengths to which people you know have gone in the past to find righteousness.

- What are signs that a person or church is trying to enter the Kingdom through the obedience doorway instead of the love entrance?

- How should the knowledge that God loves and is near to everyone (friends, neighbors, teachers, enemies, and so on) affect our approach to them?

- What single action could you take to begin responding to today's Scripture? When will you take it? Who will hold you accountable?

ME: A LIVING AND LOVING SACRIFICE

LISTENING FOR GOD THROUGH
ROMANS 12:1-21

SUMMARY

Having systematically laid out his theoretical argument in the first 11 chapters, Paul turns now to application: how to live in the real world in light of these truths. He has argued that the wicked Gentiles are under God's wrath but the Jews are no better off without Christ—all have sinned, and thus faith is the only way to be justified. While death and slavery to sin comes through Adam; life, freedom, and victory over sin come through faith in Christ.

Now in Romans 12, we start to see how these heady doctrines play out in daily life, starting with presenting ourselves as living sacrifices of love—not just to God, but for others, as well.

PREPARATION ✠ Focus Your Thoughts

How might we treat other people differently if we did not have a relationship with God? Compare theses approaches: *(a)* treat others the way they deserve to be treated; *(b)* treat others in light of how God has treated us.

READING ✠ Hear the Word

The body and body parts are an important idea in Romans. In the world at that time, Greek thinking considered the body to be evil and only the spirit of a person was good. It was widely thought in the secular world of Paul's day that a person could never be free of sin until he was free of his body, but the spirit was a different matter. The spirit could be good and clean and beautiful. Therefore, one can readily see how people in those days might actually come up with a religion where their bodies sinned because that's what human bodies do, while their spirits remained holy and pure inside them. Paul rejected this idea completely (as did all Christian thinking). To the early Christians, the body was good and God-given, and it could be sanctified along with the spirit.

In the ancient world, it was common for worshipers to offer body parts to their god. These are called *votives*, and there are thousands of these fired-clay body parts that have been excavated at various altars of ancient gods: an ear, a hand, eye, and so on. The original readers would have had this common practice in mind when reading Romans 12. However, Paul calls us to make a living sacrifice—not clay votives, but an entire living body offered to God. He reminds us that we then become a part of the Body of Christ, each has his or her own role and place of service.

MEDITATION ⚓ ENGAGE THE WORD

Meditate on Romans 12:1-2

What sort of mercy has God shown to humans that deserves our sacrificial response?

How has Paul been speaking of the *body* so far in Romans? Imagine a mental video of yourself offering an Old Testament sacrifice as a Jew. Now visualize yourself offering this living sacrifice. What imagery comes to your mind?

Besides no longer conforming to the Jewish sacrificial system, we are also urged not to conform to the world's pattern. What are some patterns that make up the world's system?

God alone transforms our minds so we can think differently, but He uses ordinary channels. What are the ordinary means of grace God most often uses to make a worldly person think Christianly? How is God's will (as detailed in the rest of the chapter) different than how we often think of God's will?

Read the William Barclay quote, then ponder and discuss: If

our living sacrifice treatment of others would be fully modeled after Jesus' example, *how far would we be willing to go?* How can we get this kind of love?

> Love always involves responsibility, and love always involves sacrifice. And we do not really love Christ unless we are prepared to face His task and to take up His Cross. —William Barclay

Meditate on Romans 12:3-8

Some Roman Christians apparently thought they were better than other Christians. (We will see why in chap. 14.) What could make a Christian think he or she is better than others today?

Paul claims that as a part of the Body of Christ "each member belongs to all the others." Using the list of gifts in this section, describe how each gift belongs to the body more than the individual.

Read Paul's quote on page 57 from 1 Corinthians 12. Then, for each of the gifts listed in Romans 12 (prophesying, serving, teaching, encouraging, contributing to the needy, leading) describe a church body where everybody had only this one gift. Why is having and using a variety of gifts important to the ministry of the church body?

> If the whole body were an eye, where would the sense
> of hearing be? If the whole body were an ear, where
> would the sense of smell be?   —1 Corinthians 12:17

Meditate on Romans 12:9-21

In the rest of the chapter, Paul heaps one practical application
on another—listing more than 20 realistic ways of living as a
loving living sacrifice. While it is essentially a list of dos and
don'ts, these practical instructions are all rooted in one mo-
tive—love. Ponder these four questions: (1) Which of these
practical applications of a loving life do you do best now?
(You might choose to pick someone else in your group to say
this about.) (2) Which one do you struggle most to live up
to? (3) Which of these instructions is your church best at? (4)
Which one does your church need more help developing?

Privately think about someone who "mistreated" you. Paul
calls us to refuse to take vengeance, but to leave room for
God to deal with those who hurt us. Discuss the quote by Va-
lerius Maximus on page 58, a Roman author from the time of
Paul. Ponder these questions: If we act in revenge, does God
let that be the only punishment they receive? To what extent
are we stealing God's role when we try to get revenge? How
might this apply differently to individuals than to governments or nations?

> *The divine wrath is slow indeed in vengeance, but it makes up for its tardiness by the severity of the punishment.* —*Valerius Maximus*

PRAYER ☦ ASK AND LISTEN

Seek the face of God. Ask, "Lord, what are You saying to us today?"

Set aside a period of totally silent, listening prayer—asking these two questions of God: "What must I do?" and "What must *we* do as a church?"

CONTEMPLATION ☦ REFLECT AND YIELD

Open a circle of sharing for members of your study by asking: What has God said to you today through His Word? Next ask, What has God said to *us* today?

GROUP STUDY

- How are we to offer our bodies as *living* sacrifices to God?

- What spiritual gift(s) do you possess? How can you use your gift(s) to build up the body of Christ?

- How can we "be devoted" to one another by our words and actions? How can we "honor" one another by our words and actions?

- Has there ever been a time when you overcame evil with good? If so, what did you learn from this experience?

- Ask yourself: What single thing will I do this week to start changing toward what God wants in my life? Am I willing for this group to check up on me next week?

- Pray, asking God to help you be "joyful in hope," "patient in affliction," and "faithful in prayer."

THE DEBT I OWE
LISTENING FOR GOD THROUGH
ROMANS 13:1-14

SUMMARY

Christians never get out of debt. We are deeply indebted to God for everything, even though we can never pay Him back, but we feel indebted to Him anyway.

There are other outstanding debts too. In Romans 13, Paul reminds us of what we owe to others. These, too, we can never pay off. As citizens in a secular nation, we still owe honor to those in authority over us, for government was established by God. We owe our government leaders—even evil ones—our taxes and our submission. Paul said all this to Christians living in Rome where the emperor sometimes tortured and executed the very Christians who were supposed to submit.

It isn't just powerful governments we owe. We owe each other love. While Paul encourages us to pay off our financial debts, he reminds us we should never stop payment on our debt of love. When it comes to payments on our debt of love, we all have a perpetual payment plan.

PREPARATION ☦ FOCUS YOUR THOUGHTS

What good things does God bring us through other people? (And now a harder question.) What good things does God bring us through governments and government leaders?

READING ☦ HEAR THE WORD

At the time Paul wrote Romans, the persecution of Christians had not reached its peak. In fact, in some cases fleeing to the protection of Rome was a good strategy for Christians. One might argue that the *very* first Christians may have read Paul's instructions on civil obedience as sensible. Before long, however, the Roman oppression fell on the Christians (including on Paul himself) with fury, and they read this passage differently.

It would have been convenient for them to say "that was then, this is now" and resist Rome, even attempting to overthrow it or assassinate the emperor, but they did not. Under persecution, Christians took the passage just as they had under a less oppressive government: They submitted and paid their taxes.

While many Christians today face a less harsh (even friendly at times) government, it is actually more helpful to see the heroism of the more radical acceptance of this teaching by Christians hiding in the catacombs or waiting to be sent to the lions.

To capture the spirit of the original readers, plan ahead for this reading. Go somewhere catacomb-like where you can pretend you're hiding from Roman persecution—a cellar, a large closet, a small room, or a shed. Play the role with whispered talking. This may seem awkward at first, but eventually all will get the idea. In a darkened space, with only a single light (flashlight, glow stick, etc), gather around as one person reads this letter from Paul on submission. Stop and let it sink in as the physical context makes the writing take on new meaning.

MEDITATION ☦ ENGAGE THE WORD

Meditate on Romans 13:1-7

List the ways submitting to the governing authorities might become practical to the Roman readers of this book.

In what ways does God establish all such authorities? Was God in control even of getting the famous Christian-killer Nero into power? Why is this notion important to Paul's coming arguments?

Paul argues that rebelling against government authority is equivalent to rebelling against the God who established it. John Wesley tried to use this argument to persuade Americans that their rebellion against the Christian nation of England was wrong. Pretend you were a Methodist in those days—what might your class discussions have been like?

There is no distinction between a Christian authority and a secular one—both can be considered to be serving God's purposes. Think of ways non-Christians have furthered God's will on earth—especially in your own life.

Paul gives a practical reason to submit to government (fear of punishment), but he also gives a moral reason (conscience). Meditate on these two motivations for doing things like paying taxes or submitting to government. How different is the outcome and attitude in each case?

Think about the words of Jesus. Then, read Mark 12:13-17. What do you think Jesus meant by His statement?

> *Give to Caesar what is Caesar's and to God what is God's.* —Jesus (Mark 12:17)

Paying taxes can be coerced, thus we never quite know if we are doing it for conscience's sake or because we have to, but we cannot be forced (at least in free countries) to give respect or honor. Paul says, though, that we also owe this to our governing leaders. What does this mean? How can we dishonor or be disrespectful of leaders? What debt do we owe leaders in respect or honor, practically speaking? Give specific examples.

Meditate on Romans 13:8-10

While some try to drive a wedge between James and Paul on matters of faith and works, there is no doubt they agree on one matter: love is the essence of Christian living.

Based on the Mother Teresa quote, what are some ordinary ways others have shown genuine love to you? Tell the story.

> *Do not think that love, in order to be genuine, has to be extraordinary.* —Mother Teresa

Can a Christian keep the Ten Commandments—that is not break any of them? How does love fulfill the law (Ten Commandments)?

Imagine what a church would be like if everyone always and continually acted in love. Describe it. Is such a church possible or impossible?

Meditate on Romans 13:11-14

Paul suggests that judgment is nearer now than ever. How does an expectancy of the end of time as we know it affect how we live? If we were pretty sure this was our last year, how would we live differently?

Think about the James G. Watt's (U.S. Interior Secretary from

1981-1983) comment. What are your thoughts and feelings about this quote? In what ways do we personally live or not live by this principle?

> We don't have to protect the environment; the Second Coming is at hand. —James G. Watt

Paul cautions the Romans to be prepared for the "day" (the coming of Jesus Christ) is drawing near. He urges them to act morally, to avoid darkness, and put on the "armor of light." What do you think it means to "clothe yourself with the Lord Jesus Christ?"

PRAYER ⸸ ASK AND LISTEN

Seek the face of God. Ask, "Lord, what are You saying to us today?"

Sit in silence, listening for God. When you sense what He is saying, speak out what you think you hear, saying only what you hear Him saying, not your own words of response.

CONTEMPLATION ⸸ REFLECT AND YIELD

Ponder quietly what God is calling you to do. Visualize yourself obeying—as if you are watching a video in your mind.

GROUP STUDY

- What are the ways Christians today do, or should, submit to governing authorities?

- Paul claims that the government authority is God's servant. List the ways government can serve God in accomplishing God's will on earth.

- Think about and then share the similarities you see between paying off a financial debt and paying the continuing debt of love to others.

- How specifically will you increase payments on your debt of love to others? When will you do it? Who will hold you accountable?

- Paul says we are to put on the "armor of the Lord." What does your armor consist of and how will you use it this week?

- Think about the Second Coming of Jesus Christ. Take time this week to thank God for the hope and promise of Jesus' return.

JUDGING DISPUTABLE MATTERS
LISTENING FOR GOD THROUGH
ROMANS 14:1-23

SUMMARY

Some things are black and white. Other things are gray. The Bible sometimes gives explicit commands. With these, there is no question. For instance, the Bible really means we should not commit adultery, but the Bible doesn't address everything. Even in some of its commands (e.g., remembering the Sabbath), it often leaves the *implementation* up to us. This is where convictions come into play.

Christians apply the command of Sabbath-honoring in many different ways. Some insist on observing the *real* Sabbath (Saturday) while others barely even observe Sunday (other than attending church). What do we do in a church with both kinds of people? That is the focus of today's Scripture. The issue in Paul's time was eating meat (virtually all of which had been previously offered to idols) and perhaps keeping the Sabbath and other holy days. There were differences in the Roman church on these disputable matters, so Paul gave his prescription for resolution in chapter 14.

PREPARATION ⚜ FOCUS YOUR THOUGHTS

Go around the circle, and tell how your family observed Sunday when you were a child. Then, name some other family convictions (beliefs, principles, etc) you were raised with—even if your parents are not religious.

READING ⚜ HEAR THE WORD

The Roman church apparently had two factions regarding behaviors. There was a *traditional group* who wanted to keep some of the old taboos and rules. How could a serious Christian eat meat that in all probability had been offered to idols? There was one God, and not eating meat that had been offered to false gods before being sold by the butcher was a long-standing moral rule for Jews. How could a Christian compromise to eat such meat?

What about the Sabbath? Didn't God establish the Sabbath even before the Law was given—at creation? Why should Christians ignore the Sabbath?

There was also a more *non-traditional group* who considered the old taboos and rules irrelevant to Christian living. They saw no need to avoid eating meat just because some meat had been offered to idols: "So what," they might have said, "I know the idol isn't even real." They considered the old Sabbath rules a sign of old Judaism that didn't come over to the Christians who were to worship every day of the week and not consider one day more special than another. With which camp would Paul side?

Read this section by first having someone read the above introduction then a second person answer by reading Paul's reply in Romans 14.

MEDITATION ⚜ ENGAGE THE WORD

Meditate on Romans 14:1-8

Outline the logical argument for refusing to eat meat offered to idols. Then outline the other side—the reasons why eating this idol-meat is OK. Do the same for observance of the Sabbath and other special days. Make both the traditional and non-traditional arguments.

Explain the logic of how Paul used a slave/master motif to get Roman Christians to quit judging and demeaning others in the church.

Discuss the quote by Olympic athlete Vince Poscente, then connect it with Paul's use of the servant/master metaphor.

> *Judgmentalism assumes that you have the right to change someone else. Well, you don't. You only have the right to choose how you will change and behave.*
> —Vince Poscente

Paul is not addressing *in*disputable matters here, but disputable ones. How does the Church sort between absolutes and ones that are purely a matter of personal conviction? What matters do we in this group agree are clearly *in*disputable—absolutes? What are the three most pressing disputable matters in your church? How could we summarize Paul's direction here in a brief statement?

Meditate on Romans 14:9-18

Paul is not against judgment here, but against *who* gets to do the judging. In Paul's scheme of things, we all get judged. Who does this judging? Why is it dangerous for us to be the judges?

How can non-traditionalists cause traditionalists to stumble in their walk with God? Could traditionalists do this to non-traditionalists too? How?

Paul admits his own position on the meat—how does he view the thing itself: good or bad? What is the primary factor for Paul making a disputable matter either good or bad?

This chapter begins with a mind-your-own-business call, then moves to a mind-your-brother's-business call. Find the phrases and words that are evidence of this shift and discuss them.

There can be debates over idol-meat and Sabbath-breaking, but there is no debate that destroying your brother or no longer acting in love is wrong. Give examples of how both non-traditionalists and traditionalists in your church can act in love on current disputable matters.

Think about Jesus' quote from the Sermon on the Mount. How does being judgmental of others come back and effect us later? When? From whom?

> Do not judge, or you too will be judged. For in the same way you judge others, you will be judged.
> —Jesus of Nazareth (Matt. 7:1-2)

Talk about the Herbert Samual quote on how we tend to feel more virtuous (a person of virtue) when we can find and condemn apparent vices in others. How does this relate to true personal virtue (moral excellence; goodness; righteousness[8])?

> The virtue of some people consists wholly in condemning the vices in others.   —Herbert Samual

Meditate on Romans 14:19-23

Think of examples of words and actions that lead to *peace* and *mutual edification* in the Church when people disagree.

---

8. <http://dictionary.reference.com/browse/virtue>. Accessed May 18, 2009.

Paul brings the chapter to a mighty conclusion in the final verse by bringing faith into the equation—"everything that does not come from faith is sin." Explain how, in this area of disputable matters, one person can do something with a free conscience while another couldn't do it or it would be sin. Give examples.

PRAYER ⭻ ASK AND LISTEN

Seek the face of God. Ask, "Lord, what are You saying to us today?"

Silently kneel in prayer, listening for God to bring to your heart people you might tend to be judgmental of or look down on.

CONTEMPLATION ⭻ REFLECT AND YIELD

What is it I can do to change my attitude toward other people with whom I might disagree on disputable matters? In what way do I need to change my actions toward them?

GROUP STUDY

- What are some of the ways we can help those who are weak in the faith?

- Paul says that we are not to put any stumbling blocks or obstacles in the way of others (v. 13). What might be some examples of a stumbling block or obstacle that we may place in the path of another?

- Is there a conviction that your family holds that your friend's family does not? How do we distinguish between a personal preference or conviction, and a nonnegotiable given by God to everyone?

- Verse 17 says, *"For the kingdom of God is not a matter of eating and drinking, but of righteousness, peace, and joy in the Holy Spirit."* What do you think this means? How do we live a life of righteousness, peace, and joy?

- Take time to discuss what it means to "make every effort to do what leads to peace and to mutual edification" (v. 19). Then pray, asking God to help you live out the words of this verse each day.

- How has the message of Romans changed your life?

Ephesians
978-0-8341-5028-7

John
978-0-8341-5022-5

Philippians
978-0-8341-5021-8

Hebrews
978-0-8341-5024-9

1 & 2 Peter
978-0-8341-5025-6

Mark
978-0-8341-5015-7

Revelation
978-0-8341-5014-0

READ IT.
STUDY IT.
LIVE IT.

Life is busy. Take a moment to slow down and listen to God. Lectio Divina, Latin for *divine reading*, is a series of Bible studies that calls students to slow down, read Scripture, meditate on it, and prayerfully respond as they listen to God through His Word. This powerful series works great in small groups and individual Bible studies!

Order *Lectio Divina for Youth* Today!